Let's Color with Red

Sticker

Color the white shapes with matching colors.

Let's Color the Apple and Cherries

To Parents: In this activity, your child will finish coloring the apple and the cherries. If your child is having a hard time staying within the lines, suggest that he or she slow down.

Color the apple and cherries red.

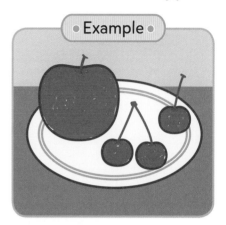

• Example •

Let's Draw Apples on the Tree

To Parents: Show your child the example of the apple tree, but explain that his or her drawing does not have to match exactly. Your child will decide where to draw each apple.

Use a red crayon to draw apples on the apple tree. Try to keep them all the same size.

• Example •

Let's Color the Chick and the Banana

To Parents: While your child is coloring, it is okay if he or she goes outside the white area. It is more important that he or she selects the right color. After your child finishes coloring, ask him or her to name the objects. This will enhance recognition skills.

GOOD JOB!

Sticker

Color the white shapes with matching colors.

Let's Color the Corn

To Parents: Encourage your child to take his or her time and color slowly in order to stay in the lines. It is okay if your child goes outside the border. With practice, your child will gain more control.

Sticker

Color the corn yellow.

Example

Let's Trace Straight Lines

To Parents: Here, your child will practice drawing horizontal lines. The lines have different lengths. Drawing long and short lines helps to build writing skills.

Use a blue crayon to draw lines from ● to ★ in the lake.

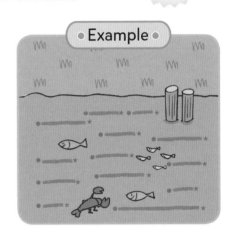

• Example •

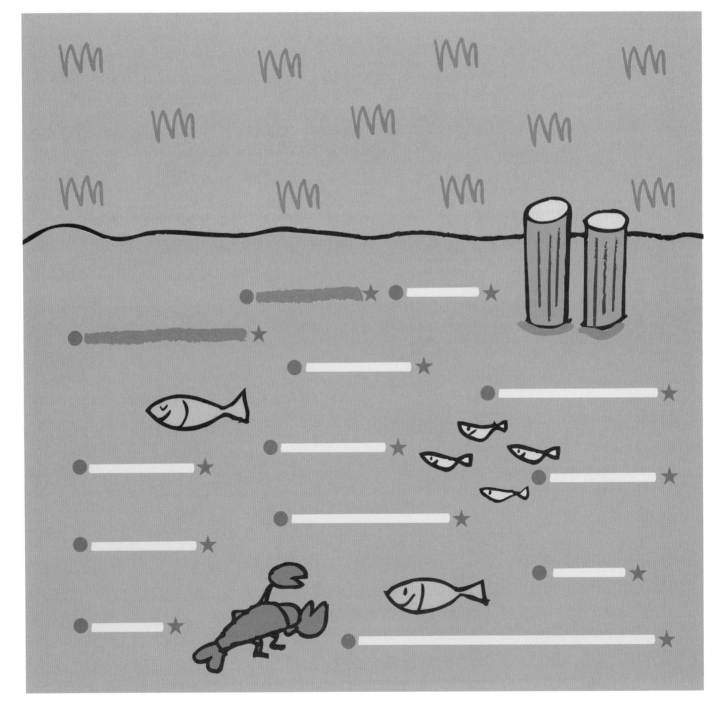

Let's Color with Green

To Parents: After your child finishes coloring, ask him or her to point to something nearby that has the same color as the pepper and the frog.

GOOD JOB!

Sticker

Color the white shapes with matching colors.

8

Let's Color the Alligators

To Parents: The alligator's jaws and tail are quite thin. Your child will need to focus in order to stay inside the lines when coloring these narrow areas. Make sure to praise your child's effort even if he or she is not able to stay inside the lines.

• Example •

Color the alligators green.

Let's Trace Straight Lines

To Parents: Make sure your child draws from the top to the bottom. Drawing vertical lines is great practice for learning how to draw letters and numbers.

Using a blue crayon, draw lines of rain from ● to 💧.

• Example •

Let's Color with Blue

To Parents: Ask your child, "What color is the shirt?" and "What color is the car?" Then, let your child choose the crayon that matches. It is okay if your child colors outside the white shapes. It is more important that she or he selects the correct matching color.

Color the white shapes with matching colors.

Let's Color the Pail and the Shovel

To Parents: If your child is having a hard time grasping the crayon, show him or her how you hold a crayon. But do not force your child to hold the crayon in a particular way.

Color the pail and shovel blue.

Let's Trace Circles

To Parents: In this activity, your child will practice drawing circles. This exercise builds focus and fine motor skills.

Trace the dotted lines around the bubbles with your finger. Then, draw the circles. Do you like blowing bubbles?

Let's Find the Squares

GOOD JOB!

Sticker

Draw a circle around each square building block.

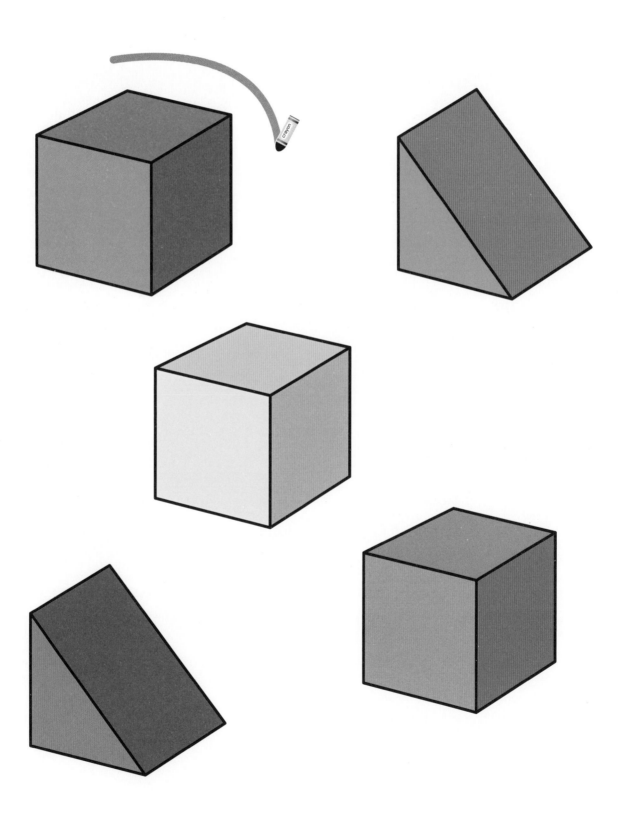

Let's Find the Circles

To Parents: In this activity, your child will practice recognizing shapes and identifying objects by a single characteristic. You will find the stickers in the front of this book.

 Sticker

Place a sticker next to each circle-shaped picture.

Let's Color the Picture

To Parents: Encourage your child to be creative and have fun picking colors for the rabbit, the bear, their clothes, the balloon, and the ice cream cone.

Color the rabbit and the bear using any colors you like.

Let's Find the Blue Balloons

To Parents: Here, your child will practice comparing and sorting objects. This activity will help him or her recognize specific objects as belonging to a group.

Find all of the blue balloons. Then, draw one big circle around them.

Let's Color the Birdhouses

To Parents: The roofs of the birdhouses are all partially colored. Have your child finish coloring them with a matching crayon. This activity is about recognizing and matching colors. Placing the bird stickers exercises your child's hand-eye coordination.

Color each birdhouse roof with the matching color. Then, place a bird sticker in the opening of each house.

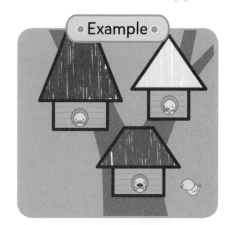

Let's Color by Number

To Parents: Before your child begins this activity, ask, "What do you think the picture will be?" to spark his or her imagination.

GOOD JOB!
Sticker

Find all the areas with a number 2. Color these areas using any color you like. What is the bear holding?

Let's Spread the Jam

To Parents: It is important to remember that coloring can be a difficult skill for young children. It is okay if your child doesn't color within the lines. With practice and encouragement, he or she will improve.

Color with a red crayon to put jam on the bread.

• Example •

Let's Color the Cabbages

To Parents: Coloring and placing stickers are activities that build fine motor skills. The stickers are in the front of the book.

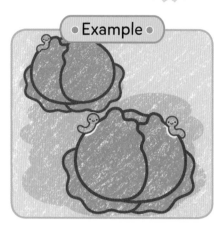

• Example •

Color the cabbages green. Then, place worm stickers on the cabbages.

Let's Color the Doghouses

To Parents: Here, your child will practice identifying and matching colors. Make a connection between the dogs in the picture and dogs in real life by talking about a pet dog you and your child have or know.

Use matching colors to finish coloring the doghouse roofs.

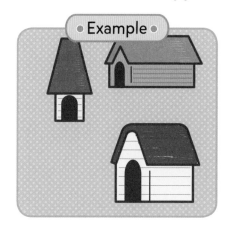

Let's Connect the Dots

To Parents: Have your child practice connecting the dots with his or her finger first. That way he or she can understand the shape of the house before drawing lines to connect the dots.

GOOD JOB!

Sticker

Draw lines from ● to ● to make a picture that matches the example. Use any color you like.

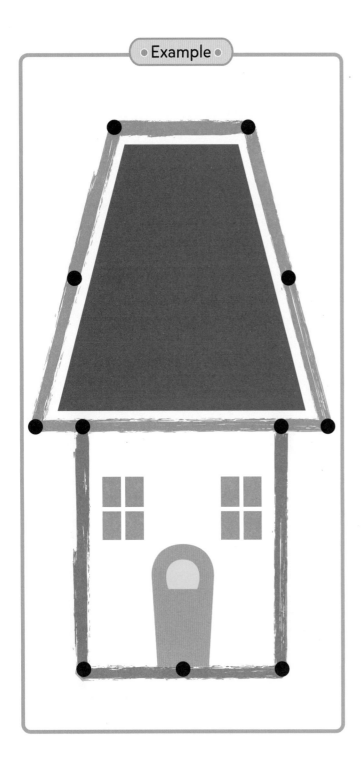

• Example •

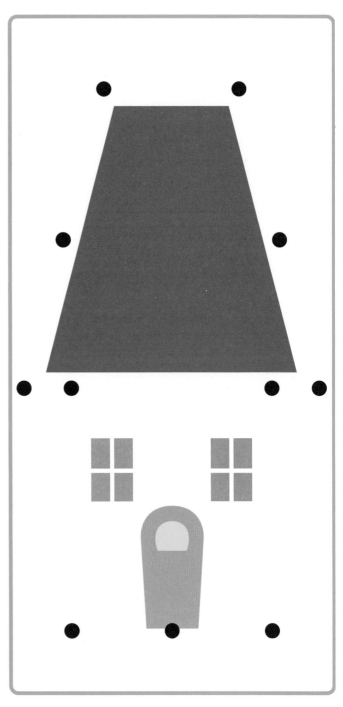

Let's Find and Color the Apples

To Parents: If your child does not immediately recognize the differences between the apples and the baseballs, call attention to the features that can be used to tell them apart.

Find the apples. Then, color them using any colors you like.

Let's Draw with Circles

To Parents: If your child can draw circles freehand, encourage her or him to draw two circles next to each another. Add lines to turn the two circles into a pair of glasses. Ask your child to draw two more circles and turn them into the tires on a car. Have fun drawing together!

Draw circles to make a picture that matches the example. Then, draw a face for the snowman. The face does not need to match the example.

• Example •

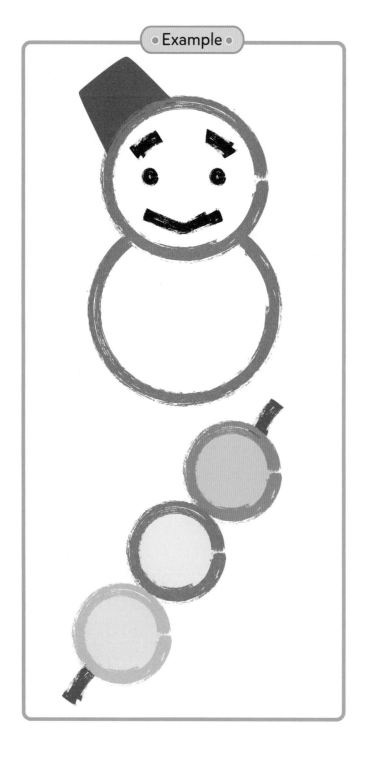

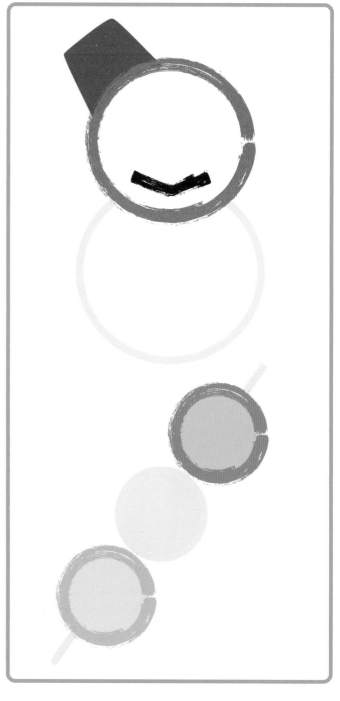

Let's Color the Eggs

To Parents: Here, your child can look at the example to identify the parts of the picture that should be colored yellow.

GOOD JOB!

Sticker

Color the egg yolks yellow.

• Example •

Let's Color the Carrots

To Parents: Some children color by making short side-to-side lines. Others are more comfortable using up-and-down strokes. It does not matter how your child colors as long as he or she is having fun!

• Example •

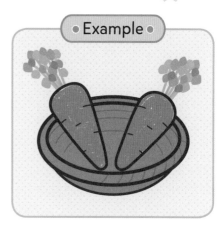

Color the carrots orange.

Let's Color the Apples

To Parents: It is okay if your child goes outside of the lines while coloring. Your child is building fine motor skills with activities like these. His or her drawing skills will keep getting better and better. Offer praise when your child is done: "Good job! Those apples look delicious!"

Color the apples red.

Example

Let's Trace the Shapes

To Parents: Here, your child will trace the triangle and rectangle that make up the house. Not only will this activity increase your child's understanding of shapes, but it will also help build writing skills.

GOOD JOB!

Sticker

Find the △ and ☐ in the picture. Trace the dotted gray outline of each shape.

Let's Color the Dog

To Parents: Before your child begins coloring, make sure she or he understands that there are two animals below and that she or he should color only one of them. This activity is good practice for matching a word with the object it refers to.

Color only the dog using any colors you like.

Let's Color the Cars

To Parents: Your child can use the same color for all three cars below, but encourage him or her to use different colors for each vehicle.

Color the cars using any colors you like.

Let's Color the Shirts

To Parents: Coloring exercises like this help your child hone color-recognition and fine motor skills.

GOOD JOB!
Sticker

Finish coloring the shirts in matching colors.

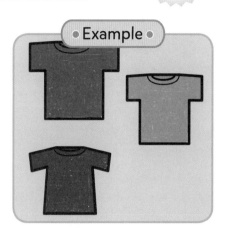

• Example •

Let's Color the Chicks

To Parents: In this activity, your child is asked to find specific objects. This will boost his or her ability to sort like and unlike objects into groups.

Color only the chicks. Use any colors you like.

Let's Color the Bananas

To Parents: Once your child has finished coloring the bananas, encourage her or him to count them.

Example

Color the bananas yellow.

Let's Color the Flowers

To Parents: Point out the colors that outline each flower. Then, let your child choose a matching crayon. The stickers for this activity are in the front of the book.

GOOD JOB!

Sticker

Finish coloring the flowers using matching colors. Then, place the butterfly stickers on the ⬤.

• Example •

Let's Color the Leaves

To Parents: Help your child understand that the picture below shows three leaves. After explaining this, see if your child colors each leaf separately or all three leaves at once. Either way is fine. Praise your child's work when he or she is done.

Finish coloring the leaves using the matching color. Then, place the frog stickers on the leaves.

Example

Let's Color the Yarn

To Parents: If your child has never seen balls of yarn before, explain that sweaters and some scarfs and blankets are made from balls of yarn like the ones in the picture below.

Color the yarn using any colors you like.

Let's Color the Balloons

To Parents: Make sure your child understands that she or he can choose any color or colors. Choosing colors is a simple way to excercise creativity and decision-making skills.

GOOD JOB!

Sticker

Color the balloons using any colors you like.

Let's Draw with Triangles

Draw with △ to make a picture that matches the example. Then, decorate them with any colors and patterns you like.

• Example •

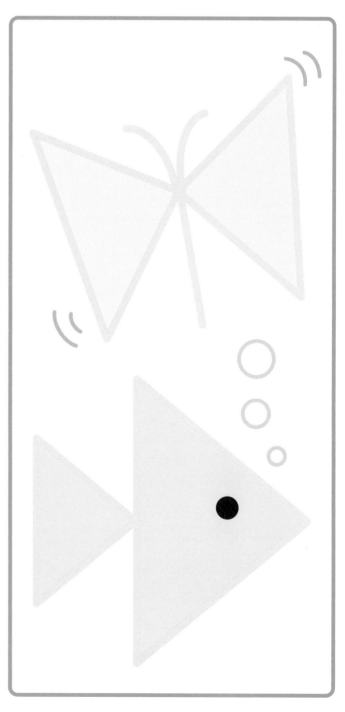

Let's Draw the Leaves' Path

To Parents: In many activities, your child is asked to draw lines from left to right. In this activity, your child will draw lines from right to left. It is important to draw all sorts of lines. It will help your child when he or she is ready to learn handwriting.

The leaves are falling to the ground. Use a brown crayon to draw lines from ● to ★.

• Example •

Let's Color the Strawberries

To Parents: The strawberries are small. That makes it more difficult for your child to stay in the lines. It is okay if the drawing is a little messy as long as your child is having fun coloring. To extend the fun, ask your child to name another red food.

GOOD JOB!
Sticker

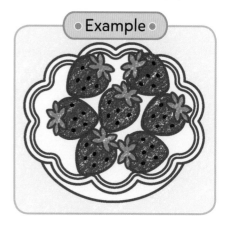

• Example •

Color the strawberries red.

Let's Color the Fish

To Parents: Point out the circles and the little gray lines in the drawing. Make sure your child knows he or she can use more than one color to decorate the fish. He or she can also draw lines or patterns on the fish.

Color the fish using any colors you like.

Let's Draw Vines

To Parents: For this activity, explain to your child that plants grow from the ground up, so she or he should begin drawing from the bottom of the page and go up.

Sticker

GOOD JOB!
Sticker

Use a green crayon to trace the looping vines. Then, place the flower stickers on the vines.

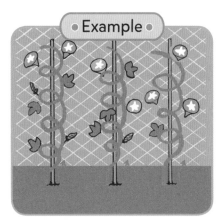
Example

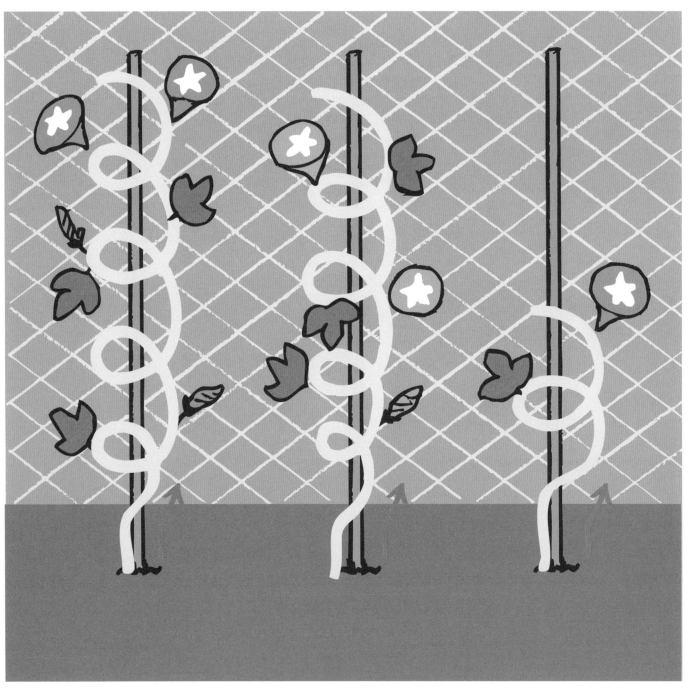

Let's Draw with Circles

To Parents: Circles are a basic shape, but they are difficult to draw. Here, your child can practice drawing circles by tracing the gray lines. Then, he or she can add straight, curvy, or looping lines to create a sun and a face. Make sure your child knows that the drawings do not need to match the examples.

GOOD JOB!

Sticker

First, trace the ◯ in each picture. Then, using any colors you like, draw lines and hair to make a sun and a face.

Examples

Let's Color the Cat

To Parents: Before your child can begin coloring, he or she will need to identify which animal below is the cat. In this activity, your child will practice sorting and comparing objects.

GOOD JOB!

Sticker

Color only the cat using any colors you like.

Let's Draw Circles

To Parents: Drawing circles is a difficult task. If your child is having trouble, make sure he or she does not get discouraged. This activity will boost your child's ability to focus and will improve fine motor control and writing skills.

GOOD JOB!

Sticker

Trace the circles from ★ to ●.

Let's Trace Zigzags

To Parents: As your child traces the zigzag lines, encourage him or her to stop at each bend before changing direction.

GOOD JOB!

Sticker

Using a green crayon, trace the zigzags from ● to ★ to add more grass.

• Example •

Let's Color the Car

To Parents: Make sure your child knows he or she can use more than one color to color the car. Choosing colors is a simple way to exercise decision-making skills and boost confidence.

Color the car using any colors you like.

Let's Trace the Frog's Path

To Parents: In this activity, your child will practice drawing a series of consecutive arcs. Make sure your child stops at the end of each arc before moving on to the next. The gray guideline for the last line ends before it reaches the frog, allowing your child to practice drawing an arc freehand.

Using a blue crayon, draw curved lines from ● to ★.

• Example •

Let's Draw Flowers

To Parents: Guide your child to draw a flower on each stem. The flowers do not need to be the same size or colors as the ones in the example.

The flowers are blooming! Color flowers on the stems using any colors you like.

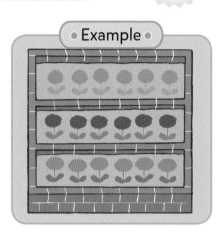

• Example •

Let's Draw Seeds

To Parents: While your child is completing the activity, explain that vegetables, flowers, and other plants grow from seeds. Once he or she has finished drawing, ask questions about what will grow in the garden. Is it a flower garden or a vegetable garden?

Using a brown crayon, draw seeds in the garden.
What do you think will grow?

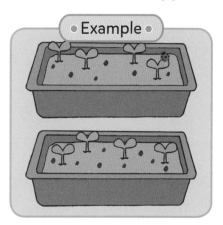

• Example •

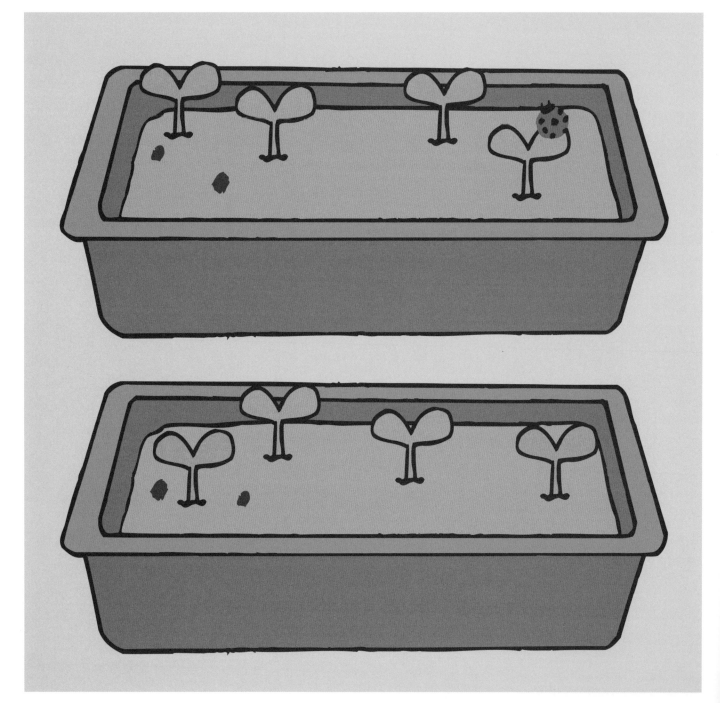

Let's Trace Circles

To Parents: In this activity, your child will practice drawing circles clockwise. Make sure your child knows where to begin.

GOOD JOB!

Sticker

Trace the circles from ⭐ to ⚫.

Let's Color the Flowers

GOOD JOB!

Sticker

Color the flowers using any colors you like.

Let's Draw with Triangles and Rectangles

To Parents: In this activity, your child will create drawings using common shapes like triangles and rectangles. Your child will also get to exercise creativity, decision making, and fine motor skills.

Trace the △ and ☐ to create a house and a rocket, like in the examples. Then, decorate the house and rocket using any colors and patterns you like.

◦ Examples ◦

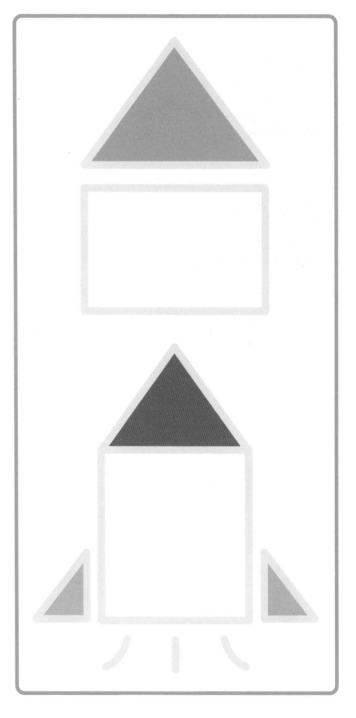

Let's Draw Seeds

To Parents: Explain to your child that it is okay to draw as many or as few seeds as he or she wants. To extend the activity, ask your child to count the seeds. Help out with the counting if he or she needs it.

Use a black crayon to add seeds to the watermelon.

• Example •

Let's Finish the Flowers

To Parents: Tracing and coloring are lots of fun, and they also help to build writing skills.

GOOD JOB!

Sticker

Trace the outlines of the leaves. Then, color them green.

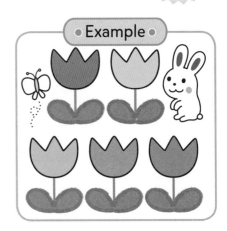

• Example •

Let's Color the Doll's Skirt

To Parents: Encourage your child to be creative. He or she does not have to color the skirt pink just because the top of the doll's dress is pink. Point out the circles on the skirt.

Color the doll's skirt using any colors you like.

Let's Draw with Circles and Triangles

To Parents: Encourage your child to look at the examples to get ideas for how to decorate the drawings. But let him or her know that the examples do not need to be copied exactly.

Trace the ◯ and △ to create a person and a piece of candy. Then, add a face to the person and decorate the candy using any colors and patterns you like.

· Examples ·

Let's Draw Snow

To Parents: Explain to your child that the example in this activity does not have to be followed exactly. He or she can draw any amount of snowflakes.

GOOD JOB!

Sticker

• Example •

Make it snow! Using any color you like, draw snowflakes in the sky.

Let's Trace the Leaves' Path

To Parents: In this activity, your child will practice drawing looping lines. In order to form the loops, the line will cross over itself again and again. It may be confusing at first. That's okay. Soon, drawing loops will be fun.

Leaves are falling to the ground. Using a brown crayon, draw the looping paths from ● to ★.

• Example •

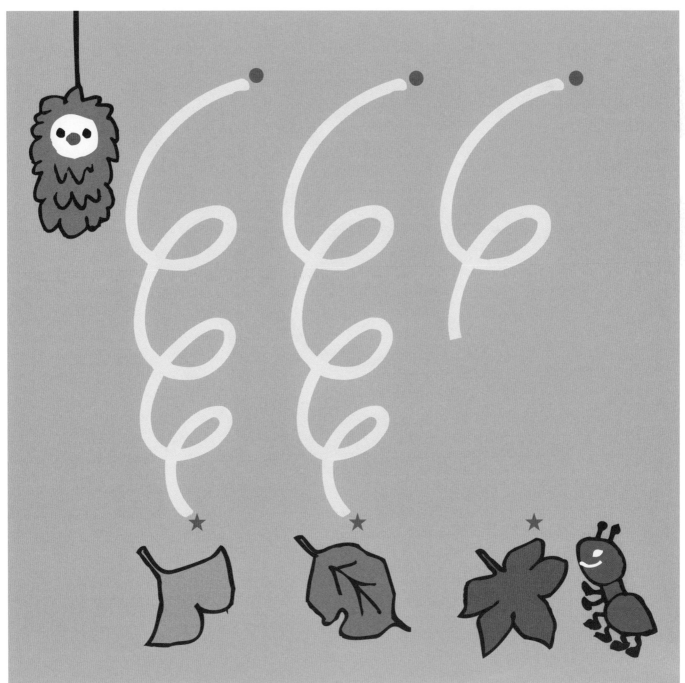

Let's Color the Lollipop

To Parents: Have your child use crayons or thick markers to color the different parts of the lollipop. After your child finishes coloring, ask, "What flavor is the lollipop? It looks tasty!"

Finish coloring the lollipop using any colors you like. Yum!

Let's Connect the Dots

To Parents: Connecting the dots in this puzzle exercises your child's observational skills. It also helps develop fine motor coordination, focus, and writing skills.

Draw lines from ● to ● to make pictures that match the examples.

Let's Color the Butterfly

To Parents: If your child cannot decide what colors to use, he or she can look at the small butterflies on the page for inspiration.

Color the butterfly using any colors you like.

Let's Color the Window

To Parents: Encourage your child to choose colors that will look good together. This will get your child thinking about color combinations. When your child is done, praise his or her work.

Finish coloring the stained glass window using any colors you like.

Let's Color by Number

To Parents: Encourage your child to color all of the shapes in each number group at the same time. This may help your child avoid coloring a shape with the wrong color.

GOOD JOB!

Sticker

Find all the shapes with a number **1** and color them red.

Then, find all the shapes with a number **2** and color them blue.

Finally, find all the shapes with a number **3** and color them yellow. What do you see?